Bessie Coleman: Queen of the Skies

by Sharon Franklin

Scott Foresman
is an imprint of

Glenview, Illinois • Boston, Massachusetts • Mesa, Arizona
Shoreview, Minnesota • Upper Saddle River, New Jersey

ISBN 13: 978-0-328-39498-2
ISBN 10:   0-328-39498-X

4 5 6 7 8 9 10 V0FL 14 13 12 11

Aletta and Jamal were talking with their parents, Ruth and Michael, at dinner one night. "I heard a story about a test pilot today in school," Aletta said. "I want to be a test pilot when I grow up!"

"Girls don't do that!" Jamal laughed.

"Dont be so quick to judge, Jamal. I have a story for both of you that will make that idea go away fast," said their father. "It's about a woman who heard somewhat the same thing from *her* brother. Her name was Bessie Coleman. We all called her Brave Bessie."

Michael continued, "Bessie Coleman was born on January 26, 1892, in Atlanta, Texas. It was a tiny town that had fewer than one thousand people. She was the tenth of thirteen children. In those days, people needed lots of children to help around the house or out in the field."

"Bessie's parents were sharecroppers, and they struggled to make ends meet," Ruth added. "Sharecroppers are people who work a farm owned by someone else in return for some of the crops."

"Times were really hard at that time," said Michael. "African Americans couldn't vote or ride in railway cars or use the same water fountains as white people. Segregation made everything more difficult for African Americans."

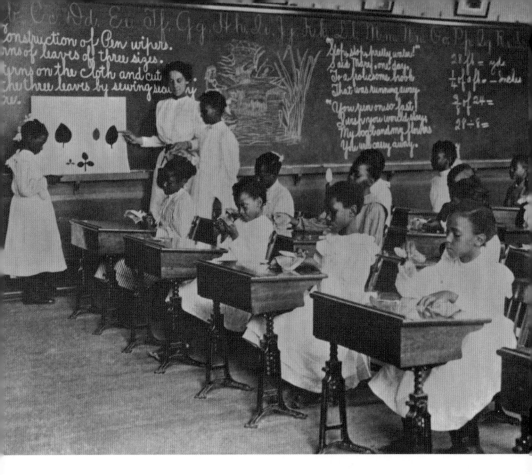

"Bessie's parents wanted something better for their family. They decided to move to Waxahachie, Texas. There were many businesses in Waxahachie. It was a place where they **foresaw** that anything seemed possible," said Ruth.

"Bessie started school at age six," Ruth continued.

"Did Bessie go to school in Texas?" asked Aletta.

"Yes, Aletta, math was her best subject. As she got older, she took care of younger children and worked in the garden."

"For Bessie, life was good," Michael explained. "She completed all eight grades at Missionary Baptist Church. However, Bessie's father, George, was angry about their life. He was tired of African Americans not being treated the same as whites."

"George was part African American and part Cherokee," added Ruth. "When Bessie was about nine, George wanted to move back to the reservation where his Cherokee people lived. He tried to talk his family into going with him, but they did not want to go. Finally, George left to return to the reservation, leaving his wife and children alone in Texas," Ruth said.

"To support the family, Bessie's mother found work as a cook and housekeeper. But during cotton harvest, everything else stopped. No matter what was happening in her classes, Bessie had to miss school and **trek** out to help in the fields," said Michael.

Ruth continued, "After Bessie finished at the one-room Missionary Baptist Church, she tried to save money to attend college in Oklahoma. However, because times were hard, she was forced to come home and get a job doing laundry."

"Did Bessie stay in Texas?" asked Jamal. "She must have wanted to get out and see the world by then."

"You're right, Jamal. Bessie was always interested in learning and seeing new things. In 1915, Bessie decided to venture off to Chicago to become a beautician. She would file and polish peoples' nails and cut and **coil** their hair. But through all those hard times, Bessie never stopped reading," Ruth explained.

Michael continued, "Then World War I raged in Europe. When it ended in 1918, many African Americans returned home to find that they were competing with white men for jobs. In the summer of 1919, a violent race riot broke out in Chicago. When it was over, thirty-eight people had died."

"How did Bessie get interested in flying?" Jamal wondered.

"Bessie began to hear stories told by pilots returning from the war. Their stories excited her. That was when she decided that she wanted to be a pilot too," replied Ruth.

Ruth continued, "Bessie applied to many flying schools in the United States. They all rejected her because she was African American and a woman."

"Wasn't she discouraged, Mom?" Aletta asked.

"Sure, she became very discouraged, Aletta, but Bessie did not give up on her dream. She tried hard to find someone in the United States who would teach her how to fly. Finally, Robert Abbott, a very successful African American newspaper publisher, advised her to save her money and go to aviation school in France. The schools there were more open to teaching women," Ruth said.

9

Michael continued, "Bessie signed up for a French language class at night, and she found a job that paid more money. Friends gave her money, too, and in November 1920, Bessie Coleman sailed off to France to attend aviation school."

Michael added, "Bessie was the only woman out of the sixty-two in her class to earn an aviator's license. She studied at the well-known school in Le Crotoy, France. She completed the ten-month class in just seven months, which made her the first African American woman in the world to do so. In September 1921, she sailed home, a very proud and happy woman."

"Suddenly, everyone treated Bessie as a celebrity. Reporters came to meet her and write stories about her. She was the guest of honor at an African American musical, 'Shuffle Along.' The entire audience, including many white people, stood and cheered," added Ruth.

"When she got home, did she get to fly?" asked Jamal.

"You bet she got to fly!" answered Michael. "Bessie knew that having her aviator's license was only the beginning. To make a living, people had to pay to see her. Bessie climbed into the cockpit, flew solo, and learned to do daring stunts like tail spins, banking, and the elegant loop-the-loop. Sometimes a plane's engine might quit right in the middle of the air. It was very dangerous. One student even died in a crash."

"Bessie realized that she had to be very skilled at entertainment flying. So she returned to France for three more months of training," said Michael.

Ruth continued "In those days, some people made a living performing tricks in the air. They were called barnstormers, and they traveled around the country performing for people. They were also called daredevils because they dared to do dangerous things!"

"Remember," Ruth reminded them, "people were just getting used to the idea that flying was possible, so seeing these stunts was very exciting! Admission was twenty-five or fifty cents. If you were brave, you could pay a few bucks and actually ride in an airplane."

Michael added, "Barnstormers jumped out of planes with parachutes, landing in fields or even on the **ridge** of a rooftop! Sometimes, even in brisk winds, they walked on the wings of a plane in flight! Daredevils especially loved cities with bridges. They competed to see who could fly under the lowest bridges."

"Imagine doing a spinning nose dive or a tail slide, where the plane falls back on its tail end. Or how about hanging by your teeth from a trapeze that is dangling from a plane, or pretending to **rappel** to the other wing without hook or **shaft**? One early stunt flyer was known for flying 'hands-off.' He would fling his arms wide open as he flew past the grandstands. In 1911, he flew over Niagara Falls," said Michael.

Ruth explained, "It was an exciting life, but it was also a hard one. Barnstormers were on the road a lot. They took great risks to do their stunts, and many died. People worried a great deal about safety, and the government finally passed laws limiting which stunts daredevils could perform."

Michael continued, "Bessie's first successful air show took place in 1922, near New York City. A reported three thousand people came out to see her do 'heart-thrilling stunts.' Suddenly, many possibilities were open to her. She considered a movie career, went to California, and bought her own airplane."

Michael went on, "Like other daredevils of the time, Bessie had accidents. She had her first accident in February, 1923. Her plane suddenly stalled in mid-air, went into a sudden **descent**, and she crash-landed. Luckily, she escaped with only a broken leg, cracked ribs, and many cuts on her face. Even so, it shook her up. It took Bessie more than a year to recover. She returned to Chicago to make a new plan, including how to get another plane."

Ruth added, "Using borrowed planes, Bessie began to perform full-time again in 1925. She performed her loops, dives, parachute jumps, and other tricks. Her daredevil stunts earned her the name 'Brave Bessie' and 'Queen Bessie.'"

"Bessie continued to barrel-roll and loop-the-loop. She gave flying lessons and lectured, and she saved her money to buy another plane," said Michael.

"By 1926, Bessie was a talented and popular stunt pilot, but she must have felt a **void**, because she was also a teacher at heart. She never missed a chance to talk to young African American men and women about the field of aviation. She encouraged them to dream big. Her dream now was to open her own flight school," Michael said.

Ruth added, "Bessie was an outspoken advocate for equal rights. She turned down invitations to perform anywhere that African Americans were not allowed. At an air show in her hometown of Waxahachie, Bessie refused to perform unless African Americans and white people could use the same entrance. Officials finally agreed."

"Did that solve the problem?" asked Aletta.

"It was a start," said Ruth. "People of all colors entered through the same gate, but once inside, they still sat in separate bleachers. It would be many years before such practices would end in the United States."

Michael continued, "Bessie lectured in Georgia and Florida and even opened up a beauty shop in Florida. She wanted to save enough money to open her aviation school. She also made her last payment on her new plane."

Michael went on, "On the evening of April 30, 1926, Bessie Coleman took her mechanic up with her on a test flight. She wanted to make sure everything was right for the air show the next day."

"Her mechanic was in front in the pilot's seat. Bessie was in the back. She did not have her seatbelt on. She was leaning over the edge, looking for good landing spots," Ruth added.

"Suddenly, the plane went into a steep nose dive, tossing Bessie out of the plane before it crash-landed. Bessie fell several hundred feet to her death. The mechanic died too," said Michael.

"Bessie Coleman died when she was only thirty-four years old," Ruth said. "She did not live long enough to realize her dream of starting an aviation school. Yet she probably helped encourage the dreams of many young African Americans."

"About ten thousand people came to her funeral in Chicago. Aviation clubs, in her name, sprang up around the country. In 1931, three of the clubs sponsored the first African American Air Show," Ruth continued.

She added, "A group of African American women pilots started the Bessie Coleman Aviators Club in 1977. In 2000, Bessie was selected to be in the Texas Aviation Hall of Fame."

"In 1992, the United States Postal Service issued a Bessie Coleman stamp. The stamp called her 'an American legend,'" said Michael.

Jamal and Aletta were quiet. "Bessie Coleman was amazing," Jamal said finally.

"People like Bessie, whether men or women, teach us a lot about courage and working hard to reach our goals," said Michael.

"I wonder if I could be a test pilot like Bessie," Aletta said.

Jamal looked at his sister. "You can do anything you set your mind to," he said.

Aletta smiled. "Maybe I'll be another Bessie Coleman!" she said.

Wilbur and Orville Wright

The same year that Bessie Coleman was born, 1892, Wilbur and Orville Wright were running a bicycle repair shop and factory.

The Wright brothers became interested in flying in 1899. In 1900, they tested their first glider, a kind of plane that floats on air. It carried only one person and had only enough lift to stay up for about 200 feet. They perfected the design the next year, but it still did not have the lift they desired. Finally, in 1902, they built a flying machine that they could control. It went 620 feet.

After that they tried to build a propeller and engine for their next flying machine.

On December 17, 1903, the Wright brothers' plane took off. For twelve fantastic, unbelievable seconds and 120 feet, they could control its flight. The age of flying had begun.